King of the Birds

by Shirley Climo

illustrated by Ruth Heller

HarperTrophy

A Division of HarperCollins*Publishers*

For our Lisas
— S. C. and R. H.

Library of Congress Cataloging-in-Publication Data
Climo, Shirley.
  King of the birds.

  Summary: When chaos reigns among the birds, Owl
declares a contest to determine who will be their king.
  [1. Folklore.   2. Birds—Folklore]   I. Heller, Ruth,
1924–   ill.   II. Title.
PZ8.1.C592Ki 1988   398.2'452897   [E]   87-47693
ISBN 0-690-04621-9
ISBN 0-690-04623-5 (lib. bdg.)
ISBN 0-06-443273-4 (pbk.)

First Harper Trophy edition, 1991.

Come and make your offering
To the smallest, yet the king

FROM AN OLD WELSH SONG ABOUT WRENS

Long ago, when the oceans were only half filled with water and just a few stars lit the sky, the birds quarreled loudly among themselves. From sunrise to sundown, the air rang with their squawks and squabbles.

Birds snatched one another's nests and mixed up the eggs. Some battled over roosts, while others fought tugs-of-war over worms. Their scraps raised such whirl-winds of dust and feathers that Chickadee was knocked upside down and Wren was tumbled from his perch.

"Stop this rumpus!" scolded Old Mother Owl. She hadn't had a good day's sleep since she'd hatched.

"Can't! Can't! Can't!" cawed Crow.

"Someone must put an end to this quarreling," Old Mother Owl continued. "Someone must decide where each bird belongs. We need a king."

"A king!" cried Gull. "Pass it on!"

Bluejay thought Gull had called "Sing!" and began to whistle. Woodpecker thought he'd said "Wing!" and flew away. Parrot started to swing on a willow limb trapeze. Most of the birds paid no attention, for Gull was known to gossip. But Wren cocked his head and wondered who might earn such an honor.

"A king," Old Mother Owl repeated. "A ruler all will obey."

"Then I shall be king," said Skylark. "Everyone listens to my sweet voice." He trilled his clear notes, over and over.

"Whee-oodle! Whee-oodle!" chirruped Wren to himself.

When Skylark had finished, Mockingbird yawned. "How dull! *My* songs are never the same." He mimicked Skylark's melody, borrowed a bar from Blackbird's tune, and whistled a measure from Nightingale's, too.

"Show-off!" scoffed Peacock. "*I* am the one with something worth showing." He strutted before them, fanning his blue-and-green plumes.

Wren ruffled his own white feathers.

"Heads are better than tails," Raven jeered. "Since *I* am so clever, *I* should be king."

11

"Respect is what's necessary," hissed Falcon. "When *I* swoop down, everyone trembles." Falcon showed his sharp talons.

Wren ran inside a hollow log.

All the other birds cried, "Choose me! Me! Me!" The racket woke hares and hedgehogs deep in their burrows and frightened the fish in the sea.

"Hush! Hush!" hooted Old Mother Owl. "Differences between birds don't matter. What is important is what makes us alike." She peered about, turning her head from front to back and back to front. "Who knows?"

Now each bird waited for another to answer. Finally Wren called through a knothole, "Birds can fly."

Old Mother Owl nodded. "Whoever flies highest and longest shall be king."

The large birds cheered. Each hoped to win the race and the throne. The small birds protested, but their timid twitters were not heard.

Wren put his head under his wing to think. Just as the contest began, an idea popped into his mind.

"Get ready!" Old Mother Owl declared. "Get set! ...Fly!"

After an hour's flight, little birds tired.

After two hours, middle-size birds wearied.

After three hours, even big birds straggled back to their roosts. Buzzard's feathers were frayed. Stork rested on one leg. Only Ostrich and Eagle remained in the match. Then, with mighty wing beats, Eagle soared high in the air, leaving Ostrich below like a shadow. Ostrich sank to the ground and refused to fly, ever again. Eagle circled alone overhead.

Suddenly Robin exclaimed, "Eagle lost a feather!"

"No, no! That's not a feather," cried sharp-eyed Magpie. "It's Wren!"

Not noticed, never missed, Wren had hidden himself among Eagle's long quills for a pickaback ride. But when Eagle folded his wings to glide down, Wren fluttered his own and flew up. He caught a tail wind and disappeared into the clouds.

All afternoon the birds watched for Wren's return. Their necks grew stiff from looking up, and a few, Flamingo and Crane among them, stretched so far that their necks were never the same again. All night the birds waited, although only the old owl could see in the darkness.

At daybreak, a speck appeared in the sky and floated gently to earth. It was Wren.

"Thank you," said Wren, bobbing his head, "for gathering to greet your king."

"Wren shouldn't win," Eagle grumbled. "He used my wings."

"He used his brain besides," answered Old Mother Owl. "One who can do that deserves to rule." So saying, she blinked and shut her eyes.

"How can we tell how high Wren flew?" Swan asked.

Mallard quacked, "We couldn't see."

"Look at my feathers," said Wren as he hopped before them. His white breast was sooty. His back was brown and streaked with gray.

"Dingy feathers aren't royal dress," said Eagle scornfully.

"They are scorched," Wren replied, "from brushing against the sun."

25

The sun! Beaks and bills snapped shut.

"And I looked down on the world and found out a secret," whispered Wren to the circle of birds. "Our earth is…an egg!"

An egg! Beaks and bills dropped open.

"The earth-egg is SO big," said Wren, spreading out his wings, "that every bird can sit peacefully upon it. There will be no need to shove or squeeze," he promised, "if all will follow my rules."

The birds stared at Wren. It was quiet enough to hear a feather fall. At last Old Mother Owl opened one eye and murmured, "Why not try?"

"Try! Try! Try!" called Crow.

One by one, large and small, the birds nodded their heads. Then, "Long live the king!" they chorused.

"Order! Order!" King Wren commanded, and he set about dividing the birds.

Some were to live on land, some on water. Some were to nest beneath bushes, others to build atop cliffs. Snow Goose traveled north while Penguin flew far south. Kiwi and Kookaburra were sent one way, Toucan and Hummingbird another. A few birds, like Sparrow, flitted everywhere. Wren did not disturb Old Mother Owl, for she was napping. So the owl still dozes while other birds sing and is awake while other birds sleep.

In time, when the oceans spilled over with salty water and stars crowded the night skies, peace reigned in the kingdom of birds. Wren never put on a topknot for a crown or wore a robe of bright feathers. He proudly kept his singed brown jacket. Never again did he venture up very high, preferring to nest near the ground. Yet, to this day, Wren carries his tail pointing straight to the sky, so that none will forget how he flew to the sun and why he is called King of the Birds.

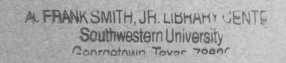

How the birds chose a king is one of the world's oldest legends. Some say that Aesop was the first to tell it. Although the story varies from country to country, it is known almost everywhere in Europe. A similar tale is told by the Chippewa Indians of North America.